BRIDGES

GRAHAM RICKARD

The Bookwright Press
New York · 1987

Topics

All the words that appear
in **bold** are explained in the
glossary on page 30.

First published in the
United States in 1987 by
The Bookwright Press
387 Park Avenue South
New York, NY 10016

First published in 1986 by
Wayland (Publishers) Ltd
61 Western Road, Hove
East Sussex BN3 1JD England

© Copyright 1986 Wayland (Publishers) Ltd

ISBN 0–531–18108–1
Library of Congress Catalog Card Number: 86–70970

Phototypeset by
Kalligraphics Ltd, Redhill, Surrey
Printed in Belgium
by Casterman S.A.

Contents

The First Bridges

A fallen tree creates a natural bridge in the Amazon jungle.

Crossing natural obstacles, such as rivers and deep valleys, has always been a challenge to people. Our first real bridges were probably trees, which had fallen across streams. These natural bridges may well have given us the idea of making simple wooden **beam bridges**. Then, when a stream was too wide to be **spanned** by a single log or plank, these early bridge builders used two or more beams to reach the other side. These planks were supported by wooden logs, called **piers**, standing upright in the water.

In areas where trees were scarce, similar bridges were built from large slabs of stone. The world's oldest surviving bridges of this kind can still be seen on Dartmoor in England. They are called **clam** or **clapper** bridges.

In China, India and South America, people developed the art of building hanging bridges from ropes and creepers. These materials do not last very long, but these early bridges were the forerunners of our modern suspension bridges.

Throughout the ages, new transportation systems developed,

Large slabs of stone form this ancient clapper bridge on Dartmoor, in England.

such as railroads, canals and main roads. Each new system needed a whole new generation of bridges, using new techniques, styles and materials to build them ever longer and stronger than before.

In times of war, bridges have always been especially important. An army can usually control a

In Papua New Guinea, simple suspension bridges are still made from ropes and creepers.

whole area of country if it can control its bridges. By destroying bridges, the advance of enemy armies can be halted, or they can be cut off from their supplies and base. As long ago as 480 BC, the young Persian King Xerxes invaded Greece by crossing the Hellespont on a floating **pontoon**. This was a bridge of boats lashed together.

Most people think of a bridge only as a structure to carry a road

This railroad bridge takes trains across the Ogun River in Lagos, Nigeria.

An aqueduct carries water across a valley.

over a river, but in fact there are several other kinds of bridges. Foot bridges give **pedestrians** a safe way of crossing roads, rivers or other dangers. There are also railroad bridges, canal bridges, and other types, such as **viaducts**. A viaduct consists of a set of arches supported by a row of piers or towers. **Aqueducts** are structures that carry water across obstacles to the villages and towns that need it.

***Far left** Walkers can safely cross this **ravine** in Ireland over a rope bridge.*

Roman and Medieval Bridges

Besides being great fighters, the soldiers of the Roman Army were great **engineers**. They became very skilled at bridge-building, and when Julius Caesar invaded **Gaul**, his army built a bridge across the Rhine River in only ten days.

When the Romans invaded parts of Asia, they discovered the secret of building a stone arch. The arch is a very strong shape and its strength led to a great change in bridge-building techniques. It enabled the Romans to build much longer

The Romans discovered the secret of building strong arched bridges.

bridges, with fewer piers between each span. Because these new arched bridges were built of stone or brick, they lasted much longer than the older wooden bridges, and many fine examples can still be seen today. In Rome itself, six fine stone bridges remain out of the eight that the Romans built over the Tiber River.

This aqueduct in France was built by the Romans in AD 14.

A song was written about this twelfth-century bridge at Avignon in France.

One of the things that helped these bridges to last so long was the Romans' discovery of cement **concrete**. They used a mixture of **volcanic soil**, **lime** and water, which would set hard even under water and enabled their engineers to build very strong piers for their bridges. In the nineteenth century it was discovered that concrete could be made strong enough to build entire bridges by reinforcing it with iron bars. Today **reinforced concrete** is one of the main materials used to build bridges.

After the collapse of the Roman Empire, the art of bridge-building almost disappeared in Europe until the Middle Ages. At about this time, an increase in the population caused a growth in the trade between the new market towns of Europe. The old bridges could no longer cope with the traffic. Travel became so slow and dangerous that the Church took on the task of

replacing the old wooden bridges
with strong new bridges made of
stone.

The famous stone bridge at
Avignon, in France, was begun in

*London's Tower
Bridge is opened for a
visiting ship.*

This Roman bridge still spans the Tiber River in Italy.

1177, and even had a song written about it. It was a good example of a medieval bridge and today some of the arches are still standing. At almost the same time, Peter of Colechurch started to build London's first stone bridge across the Thames. This magnificent bridge was supported by twenty arches. As did many medieval bridges, it had a chapel and many houses and stores on it. The bridge lasted well and served London for 623 years.

As more and more bridges were built, an increasing number of inns and markets sprang up around them. Bridges could be fortified with a strong gateway tower that could be defended in times of war. **Drawbridges** could be let up and down: they were useful in preventing enemies from invading a country or a castle. In peacetime, they could also be raised to let large ships through.

The Industrial Revolution

In the following centuries, European bridge-builders carried the art of building arches to perfection. Venice, in Italy, has about 400 bridges, more than any other city in the world. Many of these were built in the sixteenth century. One of Venice's most famous bridges is the Rialto Bridge

The beautiful Rialto Bridge in Venice houses several stores.

over the Grand Canal. Built in 1591, it has three separate flights of steps and a row of stores on either side of the roadway. Venice is also famous for the Bridge of Sighs, so called because condemned prisoners sighed as they passed over it for the last time on the way to execution.

The Industrial Revolution of the eighteenth and nineteenth centuries

It was believed that the sighs of prisoners on their way to execution could be heard coming from this bridge in Venice.

caused a great demand for canals and railroads, to move raw materials and finished goods between the new industrial towns and factories. More bridges had to be built, using new techniques and new materials.

No one had ever dared to try building a large structure out of iron. In 1779, the world's first

Iron became a very important metal for building strong bridges.

This was the world's first cast-iron bridge, erected at a place now called Ironbridge, in England.

cast-iron bridge was erected at Coalbrookdale in Shropshire. It was a great engineering achievement, using 417 tons of metal. Iron soon became accepted as a bridge-building material.

In 1826, Thomas Telford decided to use iron to build a new kind of bridge across the Menai Straits, in Wales. It was the first modern suspension bridge, hanging down on great iron chains from two towers, rather than being supported on piers.

Steel soon replaced iron in bridge building, because it is a much stronger metal. The first steel bridge was built in the United States in 1878. Until then, American bridges had been collapsing at the

Thomas Telford.

Below *The main section of a suspension bridge hangs from two towers.*

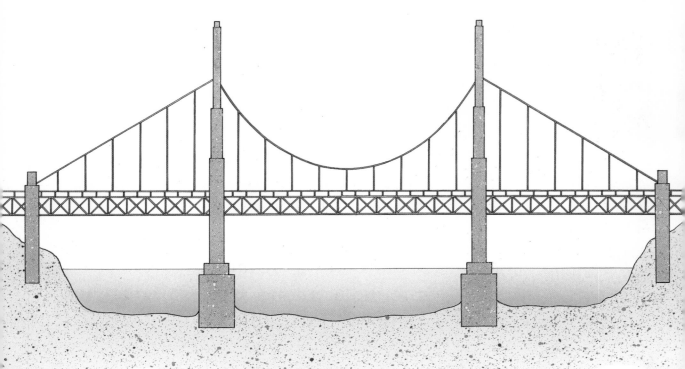

Above Building the Menai Rail Bridge in Wales, designed in 1850.

Right The tubular bridge still carries trains across the Menai Straits today.

rate of about twenty-five a year, but the strength of the new material led to much safer bridges.

The heavy tracks and trains of the railroads presented engineers with the problem of building even stronger bridges. In England in 1850, to make a rail link between London and Holyhead, Robert Stephenson and William Fairbairn built the *Britannia*, a **tubular**

railroad bridge over the Menai Straits. This was an unusual design of squared iron tubes. It proved to be strong enough to carry the great weight of the loaded trains. The Firth of Forth bridge in Scotland, opened in 1890, was Europe's first all-steel rail bridge. Instead of having a pier at each end, each beam is supported in the middle. The two "arms" of the beams are called **cantilevers**, and they meet to form a very strong bridge. The

This is an example of a cantilever bridge.

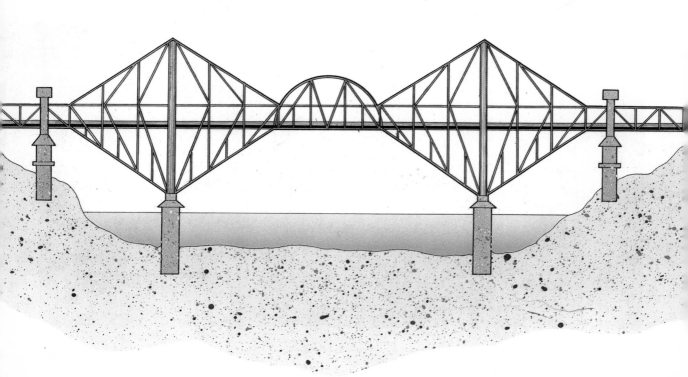

Forth Bridge can still carry modern trains at express speeds, and is so large that it takes a team of workmen three years to paint it!

It takes a team of workers three years to paint the Forth Rail Bridge in Scotland.

New bridges are constantly being built, like this one under construction in Angola in Africa.

Modern Bridges

The great increase in road traffic during the twentieth century has forced almost every country to modernize and improve its road systems, creating thousands of miles of highways. This has involved the building of many new types of road bridges, using the very latest materials.

The world's longest spans are all suspension bridges, which rely totally on the strength of steel. They vary in design, but all suspension bridges, from the most primitive rope crossings to the very latest steel structures, have three basic elements – cables, towers and **anchorages**. The cables support the weight of the **deck** and the traffic that passes over the bridge. The towers, made of wood, stone, or steel, hold up the cables, which pass over the top of them. The anchorages fasten the cables to the ground, and their weight and strength are very important to the safety of the bridge.

Suspension bridges sway in the wind. This caused a disaster in the United States in 1940, when the new Tacoma Narrows Bridge

This suspension bridge shows the suspension towers and cables.

The Verrazano Bridge in New York is a beautiful example of a suspension bridge.

started to twist in a gale. It finally broke up, ripping loose from its cables and crashing into the waters below. But the knowledge gained from this disaster led to new safer designs for future bridges. Today, the longest suspension bridge is the

Humber Estuary Bridge in England. It spans 1,410 m (4,626 ft). In the future, longer bridges will certainly be built.

Brooklyn Bridge in New York joins Long Island to Manhattan.

Many of the world's largest cities have grown up on the banks of rivers, and the separate parts of each city are linked together by a network of bridges. Bridges are the lifeline of the island of Manhattan, which is part of New York. More than a dozen bridges connect the island to the surrounding country.

Not all modern bridges are of the suspension type. They can be of

Bridges need to be kept in good condition for safety.

arch, beam, or cantilever designs, depending on the length of the span and the purpose of the bridge. Reinforced concrete is often used on major highways to make beam bridges and overpasses, and Waterloo Bridge in London is an example of a graceful concrete arch. The largest concrete arch of all spans 304.8 m (1,000 ft) of water. This is the Gladesville Bridge in Sydney, Australia. Nearby is the famous arch of the Sydney Harbour Bridge, which is made of steel. The deck of this bridge hangs by thick steel rods from a massive steel arch. The Thousand Island Bridge, linking Canada and the United States across the St. Lawrence River, is a mixture of three types of bridges. It uses suspension, a steel arch and strengthened beams.

New materials will probably be used in the near future to make bridges longer, stronger and lighter than was ever thought possible in the past. Massive bridges linking, for example, Italy with the island of Sicily will become possible for the first time. One scheme, which is already being discussed, is a combined bridge and tunnel, joining Britain and France across the English Channel. Such a bridge could be up to 10 km (6 miles) long, with separate decks for road and rail traffic. What is certain is that bridges will continue to **evolve**, and that engineers will make the best of new materials and techniques.

The famous steel arch of the Sydney Harbour Bridge in Australia.

Glossary

Anchorage A place where something mobile is secured. In this case, the bridge is anchored to the river bed.

Aqueduct A bridge that carries water.

Beam bridge The simplest form of bridge, consisting of a straight section, resting on a support at each end.

Cast iron Iron that has been molded through a heating process into a particular shape.

Cantilever A kind of beam bridge that is supported and balanced in the middle, rather than at each end. The two "arms" of the beam are called cantilevers.

Clam A simple kind of prehistoric beam bridge, made of a single slab of stone with a pier at each end.

Clapper A bridge similar to the clam, but with more than one span, supported on several piers.

Concrete Usually a mixture of water, gravel and cement.

Deck On a bridge, the surface that carries traffic.

Drawbridge A bridge that can be raised and lowered.

Engineers People who design or make machinery or construct roads, railroads, bridges etc.

Evolve To develop gradually.

Gaul Ancient region of Western Europe, roughly the same area as modern-day France.

Lime The white substance left after heating limestone.

Pedestrian A person going on foot.

Pier The upright support for a bridge.

Pontoon A type of temporary bridge, made by lashing boats or rafts together.

Ravine A deep, narrow opening between hills.

Reinforced concrete Concrete that has been strengthened with metal, usually steel mesh, to make it even stronger.

Span The distance which is crossed by a bridge, or a section of a bridge.

Tubular Tube shaped.

Viaduct A long bridge that carries traffic over a valley etc.

Volcanic soil Soil enriched by the lava of a volcano.

Books to Read

Braithewaite, Althea. *Bridges.*
New York: Cambridge
University Press, 1983.

Carlisle, Norman and Madelyn
Carlisle. *Bridges.* Chicago:
Childrens Press, 1983.

Mitgutsch, Ali. *From Cement to
Bridge.* Minneapolis, MN:
Carolrhoda Books, 1981.

St. George, Judith. *The Brooklyn
Bridge: They Said It Couldn't
Be Built.* New York: Putnam
Publishing Group, 1982.

Sandak, Cass R. *Bridges.* New
York: Franklin Watts, 1983.

Warren, Sandra. *The Great
Bridge Lowering.* Carthage, IL:
Good Apple, 1983.

Picture Acknowledgments

The illustrations in this book were supplied by: The Australian Information
Service, London 28; British Tourist Authority 8, 18, 21; Camerapix Hutchison
4, 7, 9, 24; Bruce Coleman, by the following photographers: Adrian Davis 5;
M.P. Kahl 6; Hans Gerd Heyer 11, 12; Rod Williams 14; L.C. Marigo 16; Bill
Donohoe 10, 19 (below), 22; New South Wales Government 29; The Scottish
Tourist Board 23; The Science Museum, London 20; Ann Ronan Picture
Library 17, 19 (above); ZEFA, *front cover*, 13, 15, 25, 26, 27.

Index